bake me I'm yours...

cake pops

Carolyn White

D&C

David and Charles

www.bakeme.com

I would like to dedicate this book to:

Graham, Jamie and Ella x

A DAVID & CHARLES BOOK
© F&W Media International, LTD 2011

David & Charles is an imprint of F&W Media
International, LTD
Brunel House, Forde Close, Newton Abbot,
TQ12 4PU, UK

F&W Media International, LTD is a subsidiary of
F+W Media, Inc.
10151 Carver Road, Cincinnati OH45242, USA

First published in the UK and USA in 2011

Text and designs copyright © Carolyn White 2011
Layout and photography © F&W Media
International, LTD 2011

Carolyn White has asserted her right to
be identified as author of this work in
accordance with the Copyright, Designs
and Patents Act, 1988.

The author and publisher have made every
effort to ensure that all the instructions in the
book are accurate and safe, and therefore
cannot accept liability for any resulting injury,
damage or loss to persons or property,
however it may arise.

Names of manufacturers and products are
provided for the information of readers, with no
intention to infringe copyright or trademarks.

A catalogue record for this book is available
from the British Library.

ISBN-13: 978-1-4463-0137-1 hardback
ISBN-10: 1-4463-0137-0 hardback

Printed in China by RR Donnelley
for F&W Media International, LTD
Brunel House, Forde Close, Newton Abbot,
TQ12 4PU, UK

10 9 8 7

Publisher Alison Myer
Acquisitions Editor James Brooks
Desk Editor Jeni Hennah
Project Editors Lin Clements and Jo Richardson
Art Editor Sarah Underhill
Production Manager Bev Richardson
Photographer Sian Irvine

F+W Media publishes high-quality books on a
wide range of subjects. For more great book
ideas visit: **www.stitchcraftcreate.co.uk**

contents

bring on the cake pops!

What could possibly be more fun than combining my two favourite things in life, eating delicious cake and enjoying decadent chocolate? Both of these are brought together in the fun new craze of creating lollipops made out of cake – cake pops! This book has been written for those new to creating this sweet treat and those who are looking to expand their creative skills, whether with new flavours, shapes or decorating techniques. There are plenty of sponge cake recipes and tasty toppings to choose from, and the cake pops have been themed to provide you with lots of inspiration for the whole year round – from love hearts for Valentine's Day to a snowy Christmas scene. There are also fabulous ideas for embellishing your cake pops. You will find that you can add character and personalize your pops to make them a gift with meaning or just a fun family treat.

   The cake pops have different skill ratings indicated by one, two or three pop symbols. If you are new to cake pops, make sure you work your way up to the more challenging 🍭🍭🍭 projects.

   I hope you enjoy learning to create the many cake pops in this book and, of course, tasting plenty of them along the way! In particular, you will love giving them as gifts and watching the recipient's face light up in delight.

Happy dipping!

Carolyn x

tools & equipment

Before you start, it's a good idea to check you have everything to hand that you might need. The lists here will help you make your sponge base and buttercream binding mixture, and create your basic cake pops ready to dip. Specialized tools for decorating particular projects are listed in the 'you will need' section at the start of each project.

equipment for baking

♡ Kitchen scales – to accurately weigh ingredients and cake pop ball sizes.

♡ Electric mixer with paddle attachment – to make the sponge bases and buttercreams.

♡ Plastic spatulas – to scrape out bowls.

♡ Baking parchment – to line the base and sides of baking tins.

♡ Baking tins – for making basic sponge cakes, mainly loaf tins, round, square and heart-shaped. Disposable ones can be helpful.

♡ Wire rack – for cooling cakes.

♡ Spoons – to weigh out buttercream or ganache ingredients and cake pop sizes.

tools for moulding and dipping

- ♡ Non-stick board with non-stick mat beneath – to roll out icing and to model embellishments.

- ♡ Plastic or glass microwave-safe bowls – to melt chocolate callets or candy melts.

- ♡ Microwave or double boiler – to melt chocolate.

- ♡ Wooden spatulas – for stirring when tempering chocolate.

- ♡ Roll of disposable piping bags – to pipe melted chocolate.

- ♡ Measuring spoons – to gauge cake pop sizes instead of weighing.

- ♡ Cake board with greaseproof paper – for resting cake pops in the refrigerator.

- ♡ Set of round graduated cutters – to cut basic shapes.

- ♡ Lollipop sticks – for presenting cake pops on. Use 15cm (6in) and 20cm (8in) lengths. Try wooden ice lollipop sticks too.

tools for decorating

- non-stick rolling pin – to roll out flower paste and modelling paste.
- parchment piping bags – to pipe royal icing.
- piping nozzles – for using with piping bags.
- foam pad – to cushion flower paste when forming flowers.
- mini palette knife – to cut and turn paste, and lift icing and embellishments.
- modelling tools – to create facial details, shape flowers and so on. A Dresden tool is useful for making marks on pastes, such as wood effects.
- dusting brushes – to dust edible lustre dusts on to cake pops and flower paste.
- paintbrush – to apply edible glue to attach sugar items (sable no. 2 and 4 sizes).
- dummy – a polystyrene block to support cake pops as you create them.
- paint palette – to mix colours and blend gold dust to create a paint.
- cutters and moulds – for forming cake pop shapes.
- cocktail sticks – to touch up tiny details and for dropping colour into chocolate.
- edible pen – to add decorative details.

recipes

cake recipes

Now you have all your basic equipment to hand, you can start to make your cake base. You can use almost any recipe for your cake pops, but don't choose one with nuts, fruit or inclusions that will make the pops lumpy or angular. You are aiming for a nice fine sponge crumb as your cake base. When making cake pops, the sponge cake base is baked first in a tin and then crumbled and combined with a binding such as buttercream or ganache.

golden rules for baking

- ♡ Let all the ingredients come to room temperature before you start to make your cake batter.

- ♡ Before starting to bake, read the recipe through to check the method.

- ♡ Preheat the oven and check that it is reaching the correct temperature by using an oven thermometer.

- ♡ Prepare tins before starting to make the cake mix so it doesn't have to sit. Line baking tins well with baking parchment.

- ♡ Ensure you weigh the ingredients accurately.

- ♡ Never cream your mixture on full speed – start on slow and work upwards.

- ♡ Beat the eggs and then add gradually to prevent curdling, adding a tablespoon of flour if it looks like the mixture might be starting to curdle.

- ♡ Always fold in the flour. If you do use a mixer, use a K beater on the slowest speed.

- ♡ Use a wire rack to help your sponges cool evenly.

abbreviations and equivalents

g = gram

oz = ounce

ml = millilitre

1oz = 28g approx

1fl oz = 28ml approx

tsp = teaspoon (1 tsp = 5ml)

tbsp = tablespoon (1 tbsp =15ml)

US cup measurements

If you prefer to use cup measurements, please use the following conversions. (Note: 1 Australian tbsp = 20ml.)

liquid
½ cup = 120ml (4fl oz)
1 cup = 240ml (8fl oz)

butter
1 tbsp = 15g (½oz)
2 tbsp = 25g (1oz)
½ cup/1 stick = 115g (4oz)
1 cup/2 sticks = 225g (8oz)

caster (superfine) sugar
½ cup = 100g (3½oz)
1 cup = 200g (7oz)

icing (confectioners') sugar
1 cup = 115g (4oz)

flour
1 cup = 140g (5oz)

cocoa powder (unsweetened cocoa)
1 cup = 100g (3½oz)

cornflour (cornstarch)
¼ cup = 30g (1oz)

cream cheese
1 cup = 225g (8oz)

desiccated (dry unsweetened shredded) coconut
1 cup = 90g (3¼oz)

US terms

UK	US
bicarbonate of soda	baking soda
caster sugar	superfine sugar
cling film	plastic wrap
cocktail stick	toothpick
cocoa powder	unsweetened cocoa
cornflour	cornstarch
dark chocolate	semisweet or bittersweet chocolate
desiccated coconut	dry unsweetened shredded coconut
double cream	heavy cream
flower paste	petal/gum paste
greaseproof paper	wax paper
icing sugar	confectioners' sugar
piping bag	pastry bag
piping nozzle	piping tip
plain chocolate	semisweet chocolate
plain flour	all-purpose flour
self-raising flour	self-rising flour
sugar paste	rolled fondant icing

vanilla sponge

Light and luscious, this vanilla sponge recipe will never fail to produce a great sponge base for afternoon tea or brilliant pops! If you fancy a change, for a more zingy flavour simply follow the flavour tips for a citrus version.

you will need...

- ♡ 175g (6oz) soft butter or margarine
- ♡ 175g (6oz) caster sugar
- ♡ 1 tsp (5ml) vanilla extract (or 2 tsp/ 10ml weaker vanilla essence)
- ♡ 3 large eggs, beaten
- ♡ 175g (6oz) self-raising flour

1 Preheat your oven to 180°C/350°F/ Gas 4 or 160°C for an electric fan-assisted oven.

2 Grease and line a deep 20cm (8in) round baking tin or two shallow tins and set to one side.

3 Add the butter and sugar to the bowl of an electric mixer and cream together with the vanilla extract until light and fluffy.

4 Add the eggs gradually and then sift the flour into the mixture and combine on a low speed.

5 Spoon the mixture evenly into your tins. Bake for approximately forty-five minutes if using a deep tin or thirty minutes in shallow tins, or until a skewer inserted into the centre of the sponge cake comes out clean. Cool on a wire rack.

It's easy to vary the flavours of this sponge cake. For an orange sponge, add the grated zest of one cleaned and unwaxed orange. For a lemon sponge, add the grated zest of one cleaned and unwaxed lemon.

red velvet cake

This decadent and rich dessert cake, which hails from the United States, has fast become a popular option in the UK as a fantastically naughty cake. This recipe was used to create a heavenly base for our blood red pops!

you will need...

- ♡ 150g (5½oz) soft butter
- ♡ 350g (12oz) caster sugar
- ♡ 2 large eggs, beaten
- ♡ 1 tsp (5ml) vanilla extract
- ♡ 2 tbsp (30ml) red food colouring
- ♡ 450g (1 lb) self-raising flour
- ♡ 2 tbsp cocoa powder
- ♡ 1 tsp each of bicarbonate of soda and baking powder
- ♡ ½ tsp salt
- ♡ 250ml (9fl oz) buttermilk
- ♡ 1 tsp (5ml) white wine vinegar

1 Preheat the oven to 170°C/325°F/ Gas 3 or 140°C for an electric fan-assisted oven.

2 Grease and flour your cake tins. You could use a heart-shaped tin or three 20cm (8in) round layer cake tins or two 23cm (9in) cake tins.

3 Cream the butter and sugar together in an electric mixer. Add the eggs gradually and beat for a minute longer. Beat in the vanilla extract and red food colouring until blended.

4 Sift the flour, cocoa, bicarbonate of soda, baking powder and salt together in a bowl. Fold half the flour mixture into the cake mixture, then half the buttermilk, and repeat.

5 Add the vinegar and mix into the cake mixture.

6 Spoon the cake mixture evenly into your tins and bake for twenty to twenty-five minutes, until risen and the sponge springs back to the touch, or until a skewer inserted into the centre comes out clean.

If you don't have buttermilk, you could use 1 tablespoon (15ml) white wine vinegar or lemon juice and mix this with enough milk to make up to 250ml (9fl oz). Leave for ten minutes and then use the quantity required in the recipe.

coconut sponge

This is a lovely recipe, which thanks to the coconut creates a tasty and beautifully moist sponge cake. Putting the desiccated coconut into boiling water will rehydrate it ready for baking.

you will need...

- 225g (8oz) soft butter
- 225g (8oz) caster sugar
- 50g (2oz) desiccated coconut soaked in 150ml (5fl oz) boiling water
- 1 tsp (5ml) vanilla extract
- 200g (7oz) self-raising flour
- 25g (1oz) cornflour
- ½ tsp baking powder
- 4 large eggs, beaten

1 Preheat the oven to 180°C/350°F/Gas 4 or 160°C for an electric fan-assisted oven.

2 Grease and line a deep 20cm (8in) square cake tin or two shallow 21cm (8¼in) round cake tins.

3 Cream the butter and sugar together in an electric mixer until light and fluffy. Add the desiccated coconut and vanilla extract – the coconut will have absorbed all the water.

4 Sift the flour, cornflour and baking powder together in a bowl. Beat the eggs into the cake mix gradually and then fold in the flour mixture.

5 Spoon the cake mix evenly into your tins and bake for thirty-five to forty-five minutes if using a deep tin or twenty-five minutes in shallow tins, or until a skewer inserted into the centre comes out clean.

chocolate buttermilk cake

Who can resist a chocolate cake? This one is easy to make and is rich and delicious, especially when combined with a chocolate ganache binding.

you will need...

- ♡ 165g (6oz) soft butter
- ♡ 300g (10½oz) caster sugar
- ♡ 2 tsp (10ml) vanilla extract
- ♡ 3 eggs, beaten
- ♡ 200g (7oz) plain flour
- ♡ 65g (2½oz) self-raising flour
- ♡ 70g (2½oz) cocoa powder
- ♡ 1 tsp baking powder
- ♡ 250ml (9fl oz) buttermilk

1 Preheat the oven to 180°C/350°F/ Gas 4 or 160°C for an electric fan-assisted oven.

2 Grease and line a 20cm (8in) round cake tin (or use a disposable loaf tin).

3 Cream the butter, sugar and vanilla extract together in an electric mixer until light and fluffy. Add the eggs gradually, incorporating them well after each addition.

4 Combine all the dry ingredients and then fold them into the mixture, alternating with the buttermilk.

5 Spoon the cake mix evenly into your tin and bake in the oven for an hour, checking that a skewer comes out clean when inserted into the deepest part of the cake. Leave to cool for five minutes before turning out of the tin.

When cool, try brushing your chocolate buttermilk cake with sugar syrup to add flavour and give a soft and tender crumb.

devil's cake

This cake can be made in no time at all from our special pre-mixed pack – just add oil and water, mix and it's ready to bake. Vanilla sponge is also available as a pre-mixed pack. See Suppliers for details of obtaining packs or order online at: www.cakes4funshop.co.uk

binding recipes

Bindings and frostings are mixed with the cake crumb so that cake pops can be formed into balls and other shapes. It's easy to add different colours and flavours too.

you will need...

- 500g (18oz) icing sugar
- 250g (9oz) salted butter (must be soft)
- ½ tsp (2.5ml) vanilla extract (or 1 tsp weaker vanilla essence)
- about 2½ tbsp (35ml) water

vanilla buttercream

Vanilla buttercream is so easy to make and is the perfect binding for many of the cake pop recipes. It can also be used as a topping. Use salted butter for a rich, creamy but slightly less sweet buttercream.

1 Sift the icing sugar on to the butter in an electric mixer, add the vanilla extract and beat on slow.

2 Gradually increase the speed to high until the mixture is light and fluffy. Add the water until the desired consistency is reached.

Buttercream can be combined with citrus for extra flavour. For either a lemon or orange buttercream, add ½ tsp (2.5ml) of a good-quality lemon or orange oil. Alternatively, zest a cleaned, unwaxed lemon or orange and mix into the buttercream.

chocolate buttercream

This chocolate buttercream is a perennial favourite. It's best to buy the chocolate in callet form, as the small pieces melt more evenly. Strawberry and caramel-flavoured chocolates are also available.

you will need...

- ♡ 125g (4½oz) dark chocolate callets
- ♡ 250g (9oz) soft butter
- ♡ 250g (9oz) sifted icing sugar

1 Put the couverture chocolate callets in a plastic jug and place in a microwave on medium for two minutes and then in short bursts until it is melted (see also Tempering Chocolate).

2 Cream the soft butter and icing sugar in an electric mixer on slow. Add the liquid chocolate, mixing and beating on high until soft and light.

---

lemon cream cheese frosting

The addition of cream cheese and lemon in this frosting makes it smoothly rich yet fresh and zesty – a real winner.

you will need...

- ♡ 30g (1oz) soft butter
- ♡ 80g (3oz) cream cheese
- ♡ 1 tsp finely grated lemon zest
- ♡ 240g (8½oz) sifted icing sugar

1 Cream the butter, cream cheese and lemon zest in a small bowl with an electric mixer until light and fluffy.
2 Gradually beat in the icing sugar.

dark chocolate ganache

A ganache is a rich mixture of chocolate and cream used for a frosting or filling. For this recipe you can use any good-quality dark or plain chocolate – see Chocolate & Coatings and also Microwave Tempering. These instructions can be used for various chocolate flavours.

you will need...

- ♡ 500ml (18fl oz) double cream
- ♡ 120g (4oz) glucose
- ♡ 500g (18oz) dark or plain chocolate callets

1 Put the cream and glucose together in a plastic bowl in a microwave and bring to the boil.

2 Pour over the chocolate callets in a bowl and stir until smooth. Allow to cool. Use the following day.

white chocolate ganache

Make this in the same way as the dark version. You could also use strawberry or caramel-flavoured couverture chocolate.

you will need...

- ♡ 250ml (9fl oz) double cream
- ♡ 60g (2oz) glucose
- ♡ 500g (18oz) white or milk chocolate callets

royal icing

Royal icing is used in small amounts to pipe eyes and fine details, and also to fix embellishments. You can make your own, described below, or use a commercial powder mix. You can use fresh egg white or dried egg powder. If you are using a dried powder, add water and soak for a minimum of forty minutes or even overnight in a refrigerator. When ready to use, strain the mixture first.

you will need...

- ♡ 500g (18oz) sifted icing sugar

- ♡ 2 egg whites, or 15g (½oz) dried egg albumen powder mixed with 75ml (2½fl oz) water

ready, steady, go...

Save time by keeping a box of ready-made royal icing powder in the store cupboard. You can make up very small amounts and use immediately. Just follow the manufacturer's instructions.

1 Sift the icing sugar directly into a bowl and add the fresh egg whites or strained soaked dried egg whites. Using an electric mixer, mix slowly on a low speed for five minutes until the icing has reached a 'stiff peak' stage.
2 It is now ready to use or store. It can be stored in the refrigerator for two to three days covered with cling film and in a lidded box. To colour the icing, simply add some drops of colouring with a cocktail stick and mix well, adding more drops until the shade is as you desire.

techniques

making cake pops

The instructions here describe the basic steps for making any type of cake pop. The quantities are for twelve round pops.

1 Trim any crispy or darker edges from your cake so you are left with the softest part. Take 240g (8½oz) and crumble it to a fine crumb – you can use a food processor on pulse or do by hand.

2 Prepare 120g (4oz) of binding, such as buttercream, frosting or ganache. Use a spoon to combine the cake crumb and the binding to create a firm mix.

3 To create the cake balls, you have two options. If you have a measuring spoon set, choose the tablespoon size and spoon out two level tablespoons. Alternatively, use scales to weigh

a 30g (1oz) amount and then roll to a smooth cake ball. Once you have your first cake ball, it's really easy to use this as a size guide so you don't have to keep referring back to the scales to weigh each one. The sizes used in this book are: 10g (⅓oz) 15g (½oz), 20g (¾oz), 30g (1oz) and 40g (1½oz). See overleaf for creating other shapes.

4 Roll the cake pop amounts together into a smooth ball. This will create a ball size of approximately 30g (1oz), which is the one used most in this book.

5 With a cake pop stick, make an indentation for the stick to go into and withdraw the stick.

6 Place the cake on greaseproof paper and put into the refrigerator for up to an hour to firm. Do this with care, as sometimes the pops can lose their shape slightly. For shapes with a flat side, lay on the flat side. For round balls, place hole-side down where possible. For mini wedding cakes, stick the two circles together with melted chocolate and place hole-side down.

7 Prepare your chocolate or coating to dipping consistency. Fill a disposable plastic or parchment piping bag with chocolate or coating, then snip off the tip, pipe straight into the hole and immediately insert a cake pop stick. Place in a polystyrene block and do the next pop. The coolness of the cake and warmth of the chocolate will firm together, ensuring the stick is well secured. The cake pops are now ready for dipping and decorating – see Chocolate & Coatings.

freeze with care...
Once formed, fifteen minutes in a freezer can firm up cake pops, but let them come to room temperature before dipping, otherwise cracks can form. You can also prepare pops in advance and freeze them in an airtight container. Defrost for a while before dipping.

shaping cake pops

Cake pops can be shaped into almost any form you like. Those used in the book include rounds, ovals, rectangles, teardrops and cones. You can also use cutters for more unusual cake pops, such as hearts, stars, flowers and even baby feet.

cake pops troubleshooting

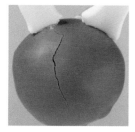

cake pops cracking – this can happen when cake pops are kept in the freezer for too long. When the sponge then expands in a warmer temperature, the coating can crack.

solution: don't put cake pops in the freezer for more than fifteen minutes – use a refrigerator if possible.

blooming on chocolate – this is where white or dull patches occur within the coating, usually because the chocolate has been heated too much and moved out of 'temper'.

solution: take care when heating chocolate, checking it frequently to ensure it is only just melted – see Tempering Chocolate.

coating not setting – this usually occurs when chocolate has not been kept within temper, so it stays sticky for a long time.

solution: re-temper the chocolate and re-dip your pops

chocolate or coating too thick – coating that is too thick will make smooth coverage difficult when dipping pops.

solution: mix a couple of tablespoons of vegetable oil into the coating before dipping your pops.

pops falling off the stick – this is normally because there isn't enough chocolate in the stick hole.

solution: make a hole with the lollipop stick, pipe chocolate fully into the hole and then re-insert the stick. Chill in the refrigerator to set before dipping.

cake grease colouring the stick – this is usually due to the fat being drawn out of the cake pop via the stick if the pops are a few days old.

solution: ensure the coating fully coats the shape at the very top of the stick to fully encase the whole pop. This limits the problem but won't stop it completely – although most cake pops will have been eaten long before this!

oil seeping from the cake – this can be due to the coating not fully covering the cake pop and sealing it, probably because the pop hasn't been tapped and moved around after dipping

solution: ensure you tap the base of the stick firmly downwards on a firm surface to help move the coating over the pop, and then turn upside down and swirl above the bowl of coating to allow the excess to come off.

chocolate & coatings

There are many options for coating cake pops and this section describes those used for the projects in this book. I love using Belgian chocolate callets, which is a couverture chocolate prepared as little buttons. They taste superb and produce great results. You can get callets in reasonably sized quantities and in a range of types, such as white, milk and dark chocolate, and different flavours, such as strawberry, orange, lemon, caramel and cappuccino. You can also buy chocolate paste in these same flavours. See Suppliers at the back of the book.

commercial callets...

Small buttons of high-quality chocolate in various flavours are easy to melt and readily available – see Suppliers.

You really need to work with a good-quality couverture chocolate designed for chocolate work or a candy coating to get the best results. A couverture chocolate is of a high quality and contains extra cocoa butter. If using a bar of chocolate bought in a grocery store, you will find it's just not possible to temper it and it will easily seize up or burn. Remember that a bar of chocolate has been created to be eaten just as it is, not to be melted and used in the creation of something else! If you do choose to use a chocolate bar, ensure you break the blocks into very small, even-sized pieces or chop them to a finer size, as it's important that it all melts evenly. Reserve some of the chocolate in case it overheats and you need to add some fresh chocolate into your main bowl.

When preparing chocolate or other coatings, use a small, deep bowl, as this will allow you to get good coverage on your cake pops. Don't attempt to dip in a shallow bowl.

tempering chocolate

Tempered chocolate can be used for dipping and to attach decorations and embellishments to your cake pops. It can also be used in a piping bag to fix the cake pop sticks in place – simply pipe chocolate into the holes that the sticks are to go into.

Belgian chocolate callets...

I love delicious Belgian chocolate callets and use them for ganache, buttercream and dipping.

Tempering chocolate is an art in itself. There are many professional and quite complicated methods of tempering chocolate that achieve a very high-quality result. However, we don't need elaborate methods for our fun little cake pops, so a much simpler method is described here.

When you buy couverture chocolate, it comes in little buttons known as callets. To create these buttons it has already been tempered at manufacture, so I normally use a method based on microwave tempering, which really doesn't take the chocolate out of the 'temper' it is already in. However, although this method is easy, quick and reliable, you must take great care.

If a coating is too thick, you can get good results by adding a couple of tablespoons of vegetable oil to each batch. This really isn't detectable in the taste and creates a beautifully smooth coating.

microwave tempering

While this is a great way to temper small amounts of chocolate, try not to do it with less than 250g (9oz) of chocolate. If you use less, the chocolate is far more likely to burn.

1 Add your small couverture chocolate callets to a microwave-safe bowl and heat in a burst of medium heat for a maximum of thirty seconds to start with and then remove and stir. It's easy to think you can leave it for double the time, but it melts so quickly that this will cause the batch to be ruined, so be very careful to do it in short bursts.

2 As you see signs that the chocolate is beginning to melt, reduce the time in the microwave to five to ten seconds at a time. When you can see only a few remaining blobs of chocolate, remove from the microwave totally and keep stirring until the residual heat within the bowl has melted the last remaining pieces.
3 If you need to add any more heat, do it in very short bursts of a couple of seconds and stir very thoroughly to ensure the heat is well dispersed. By this point you will have reached a working temperature. Technically the chocolate has been melted to such a slight degree that it will not have come 'out of temper'.

well-tempered chocolate will:

♡ have a high gloss

♡ be resistant to warmth (not be tacky at room temperature)

♡ have a wonderful smell

♡ have a good snap when you bite into it

♡ taste smooth on the tongue

poorly tempered chocolate will:

♡ look dull

♡ feel soft or flexible to the touch

♡ be vulnerable to warmth (tacky at room temperature)

♡ have a fat bloom or white streaks in the surface

double-boiler tempering

If you don't have a microwave, you can melt chocolate the old-fashioned way using a double boiler, sometimes called a bain-marie or water bath. You will need to take great care that you do not overheat the chocolate.

1 Put two-thirds of the chocolate in a heatproof glass bowl over a saucepan of boiling water on an oven hotplate. Do not let the water come into contact with the bottom of the bowl or any steam or water reach the chocolate. Melt the chocolate slowly.

2 Once it has melted, remove from the heat, add the remaining callets and keep stirring until all are melted. This brings the temperature down to a working level.

3 To test the chocolate, dip a clean palette knife into it and allow it to set for two to three minutes. If it's shiny, snaps easily and has set quite hard, then it's ready for use.

chocolate rescue...

If you overheat your chocolate, add additional couverture chocolate to bring down the temperature. It's vital to keep stirring as you do this. If you are worried about correct temperatures, you could check with a cooking thermometer. Chocolate should be heated to no more than 31°C (87.8°F) for dark, 30°C (86°F) for milk and 29°C (84.2°F) for white chocolate.

avoiding bloom

Blooming is a term used to describe a greyish film on chocolate, and there are two types that can occur – sugar bloom and fat bloom. Sugar bloom is dry, can be slightly grainy and does not melt to the touch, whereas fat bloom feels greasy and will melt when touched.

fat bloom

This occurs when chocolate used has gone 'off temper'. It can be caused by incorrect tempering when creating your dipping chocolate, or warm storage conditions thereafter. It can also be caused by adding an incompatible fat to cocoa butter – vegetable oil usually gives good results. To correct a fat bloom, use a direct heat source such as a hair dryer *very gently* at a distance away from the bloom to melt the crystals and the appearance of bloom will disappear. Do this only in *extreme* circumstances and with care, as cake pops are highly sensitive and can be damaged easily.

sugar bloom

This is caused by moisture or beads of condensation forming on the surface. Once dipped don't refrigerate your cake pops, as this can lead to moisture. It's not possible to correct sugar bloom once it has occurred.

colouring chocolate

Chocolate with a colour is usually based on white chocolate that has flavours and colours added to it. Treat all coloured chocolate as white chocolate and reduce timings by half, as the high content of cocoa butter and sugars within the chocolate means it can burn very easily.

cool, dry storage...

Chocolate-topped cake pops are best stored in dark, cool and dry conditions. If left near a heat source or direct sunlight, the chocolate can melt quite quickly.

Once tempered, use a powder or non-water-based gel colour to colour the chocolate. If you are using powder, it's best to mix it first with a little melted cocoa butter before blending it into the chocolate. If you feel the coating is too thick, add a little vegetable oil.

using candy coatings

There are many makes of candy coatings or candy melts that are fantastic to work with, as you simply melt them in the microwave and begin dipping. If you find they are a little too thick to work with, simply add a couple of tablespoons of vegetable oil and stir well. They also come in a great range of flavours, such as mint chocolate, peanut butter and strawberry! You can get fantastic true whites and blacks rather than laboriously colouring chocolate to achieve these more difficult shades.

dipping cake pops

Dipping cake pops is easy – just ensure that your dip is melted properly and that oil has been added. Check that the bowl you are using is deep enough to dip the cake pop shape fully into the coating.

1 Take your cake pop and dip it completely in the coating. Tilt the bowl if necessary to achieve the depth needed to coat properly.

2 Raise the pop from the coating and gently tap the stick on the side of the bowl, while keeping the cake pop above the coating so the excess falls back into the bowl.

If you have left-over chocolate, pour it on to baking parchment or cellophane and allow it to cool. Snap it into little pieces and store in a bag until needed.

3 Remove from the bowl and tap once or twice with the base of the stick on the work surface just to ensure the coating has worked down and meets the stick beneath the pop. Then hold it back above the bowl and twist your wrist to remove any further excess. Once the flow from the pop reduces, tap once more and turn upright.

4 After the initial coating, if you want to dip into any sprinkles or sugars, do this quickly now, before the coating becomes touch dry. Set the dipped cake pop aside in a polystyrene block to firm.

decorating & modelling

There are so many exciting and enjoyable ways of decorating cake pops. A variety of materials can be used for modelling embellishments and in this book modelling paste, sugar paste, chocolate paste and flower paste are used.

using royal icing

Royal icing is perfect for piping fine details and to fix embellishments in place, and is easily coloured. You can make your own or buy commercially prepared icing.

Place a spoonful of the icing in a small bowl and add a few drops of water until it reaches a softer piping consistency. Put the correct nozzle into a parchment piping bag and then add a quantity of the royal icing. A no. 1 or 1.5 nozzle will be most useful. To colour royal icing, add a few drops of colouring and mix well until the desired shade is reached. Royal icing can also be painted with edible lustre dust, as the Love Hearts cake pops were.

using flower paste

This is a fantastic medium to work with for small, delicate pieces, as you can roll it really finely. It's available in any colour you could wish for. It's best to buy it ready-made. It will dry to a strong and hard finish, which is ideal for delicate items such as flower blossoms and snowflakes. It dries quickly, so cut off only as much as you need and keep the rest sealed in the bag it comes in.

using modelling paste

This paste dries almost as hard as sugar paste and retains its shape well, so is perfect for modelling. You can use a ready-made paste from cake-decorating shops or create your own by blending 50/50 of sugar paste with flower paste, or blending CMC (carboxylmethyl cellulose) with sugar paste.

Roll out the paste and cut into strips. The ribbon curls on the Perfect Presents pops were created by wrapping the strips around a pop stick. Cutters can be used for more detailed shapes.

using sugar paste

Sugar paste, or rolled fondant icing, is a thick, easily shaped and coloured icing. It can be made from scratch but it's more convenient to buy it ready-made from supermarkets and cake-decorating shops. It comes in a fantastic array of colours. We mainly use it to cover cake bases and dummies.

using chocolate paste

This matches the chocolate coatings made from Belgian chocolate and tastes delicious! It comes in all the Belgian chocolate flavours mentioned before and I love to use it on the pigs' ears for the Farmyard Fun pops, as the colour matches perfectly. Use this paste in the same way as modelling paste but be quick with it, handling it as little as possible.

Simply knead the paste and the warmth of your hands and the movement help to activate the glycerine and glucose in the paste so it is smooth, pliable and crack-free when rolled. For modelling embellishments it's a little soft, so add a teaspoon (5ml) of CMC (carboxylmethyl cellulose), which is a strengthener, to every 450g (1lb) of paste.

embellishments

The sky's the limit when it comes to embellishments, those little features that bring cake pops to life, and the additions that add a wow factor, such as edible glitters and lustre dusts. Try using sprinkles, sweets and mini pretzels for great finishing touches. Specialist products are also available, such as edible gel, which can be used to attach sugar details and to add realism to ghoulish pops.

making eyes

Most eyes can be created by piping dots of black royal icing with a no. 1.5 nozzle, which is the quickest method to add character to your pops. If you need to add extra expression, cut out a small circle of white flower paste and pipe on a pupil. Have some eyes looking to the left, right or up or down to add interest to arrangements.

making ears

From sweet teddies to porky pigs, our pops feature a range of different ears, but the technique is basically the same. Take a small ball and roll it into a teardrop shape. Flatten and pinch this to shape, then attach it to the cake pop with sugar glue or royal icing. For a rabbit, model a longer, thinly pointed shape and fill the centre of the ear with a white or pink section to give a really cute look.

making noses

Little cut-out shapes of modelling paste make great noses – from fat round circles for a pig's snout, through to mini hearts on a cute spring lamb. Use the small, round end of a ball tool to impress nostrils into a snout.

making bows

Cut three thin strips of paste and shimmer with lustre dust. Fold one strip over at both ends and fix in the centre with edible glue. Wrap the second strip over the centre of the two-loop section and glue. Cut a diagonal line through the remaining strip and attach the two flat ends beneath the bow with glue, adjusting the tails for an even look.

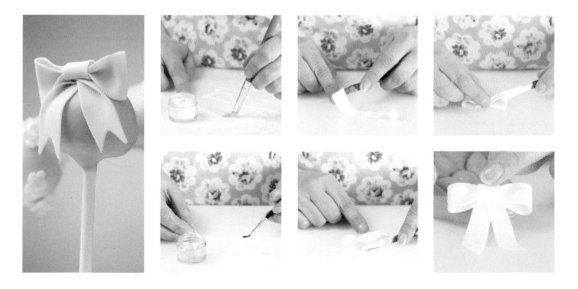

making flowers

A variety of flower-shaped cutters can be used to create floral shapes, in particular a marguerite/daisy cutter, or even cheat and buy lots of ready-made sugar flowers. You could, of course, create your own flowers by modelling or piping. Flower centres can be piped in royal icing.

adding to embellishments

A huge part of the fun in making cake pops is the chance to be really creative with the embellishments you use.

lustre dusts

These ultra-shiny edible dusts give a luxurious sheen when applied with a large, flat-headed brush and worked into modelling paste. There are also spray alternatives that work well. Try spraying your pops with a silver or pearl effect, but don't have other pops sitting too close by, as the dust floats in the air and can coat things you weren't expecting it to! Isopropyl alcohol or clear alcohol can be mixed with lustres so they can be applied as a painted decoration. Any alcohol can be used, even gin or vodka!

glitters

Edible glitter for a hint of sparkle is normally applied from a height above the pops. If you want a more concentrated effect, such as for a reindeer nose or the tip of a devil's tail, paint the item with edible glue and then apply a liberal sprinkling of glitter.

sprinkles & non pareils

There are fantastic sprinkles, sugar strands, vermicelli strands and all sorts of sugar decorations that will really add to your cake pops. Try pearl balls, dragees, sugar balls, edible hearts and stars.

attaching embellishments

Throughout the book various mediums have been used to attach ears, noses and eyes. Royal icing, sugar glue, edible gel and melted chocolate all work well.

presentation & storage

Cake pops can be presented in so many exciting ways and the presentation projects throughout the book give some great ideas on how you can arrange your pops for a special gift.

wrapping cake pops

Think about how you want to present the cake pops when choosing the design. If they are to be wrapped in cellophane, choose simpler designs to ensure delicate embellishments are not broken when wrapping. Items like snowflakes and reindeer antlers are probably best not wrapped and gift boxed, whereas the sweet treat pops or glitter balls would be perfect.

boxing cake pops

A lovely gift box lined with tissue paper makes a great presentation idea. Simply wrap each pop in cellophane and position them in alternating directions. Use some additional tissue paper to fill in the gaps so they don't move around. Keep an eye out for packaging that you could use to box your pops. For example, an Easter egg carton makes a great display box and a presentation box from a china cup is perfect for these little treats.

cake pop stands

Cake pop stands can be used when making your pops and also for presenting them in afterwards. Check the internet for new and exciting packaging options as the craft grows in popularity. Alternatively, convert a cupcake stand by punching holes around the outer edge.

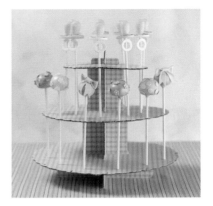

storage

Storage often isn't a problem, as most people want to eat cake pops as soon as they see them! They are definitely best eaten the same day you make them but can be made one or two days in advance if need be. The following tips will help prolong their shelf life.

- ♡ Unused cake can be cut into sections, wrapped in polythene and frozen for up to a month.

- ♡ Ensure a cake pop is fully encased in chocolate to prevent any oil seeping out.

- ♡ Store at room temperature to prevent bloom on chocolate, which can occur if chocolate is exposed to extremes of temperature, becoming too hot or cold.

- ♡ Cake pops with perishable ingredients, such as cream cheese frosting, should ideally be eaten the same day. To keep them longer, wrap individually and store in cellophane in a sealed plastic box in the refrigerator.

- ♡ Any excess sponge or frosting can be frozen as soon as it's cooled to keep for the next time you need it.

- ♡ Cake pops travel well pushed securely into polystyrene blocks.

let's celebrate

glitter balls

Reminiscent of disco days, these glitter balls will have you dancing. Eye-catching and appealing to young and old, start by choosing your favourite sponge base.

you will need...
makes 12

- ♡ 12 round cake pop bases on sticks (30g/1oz balls) – any sponge base and any binding
- ♡ 300g (10½oz) any type of chocolate or coating, melted
- ♡ edible glitter – your choice of colours

1 Dip each of your pops into the melted chocolate or coating and set aside to dry.

2 Apply sugar glue liberally, coating the whole surface.

3 Hold your pop over some baking parchment and, using a fluffy paintbrush, dip it into the glitter and tap the brush above the cake pop. Repeat until it is fully covered.

waste not, want not...
Use the baking parchment to catch any stray unused glitter and funnel it back into your glitter pot for next time.

recipes cake, binding *techniques* chocolate & coatings, dipping, glitters

pop stars

Stars and hearts are easy shapes to create and great for celebrations. Dip them into bright colours and add edible glitter for extra sparkle.

you will need...
makes 9 of each

- ♥ 9 star-shaped and 9 heart-shaped cake pop bases on sticks (40g/1½oz) – vanilla sponge with vanilla buttercream

- ♥ 200g (7oz) each red, yellow and blue candy melts, melted

- ♥ edible glitter

1 Dip three of each of the star cake pops into each colour of coating and set to one side. Repeat with the heart-shaped cake pops. Both shapes can be a bit tricky to coat, as they have lots of sharp edges, so double dip if required to get a smooth coating.

2 Sprinkle the cake pops straight away with a little edible glitter by dipping a dry paintbrush into the glitter pot and then tapping the brush gently above the pop.

make it special...
For a different look try using a multicoloured flecked candy coating.

easy does it...
Don't use a spoon or knife to apply the glitter or you'll end up with a big clump in one place – a brush gives a lovely, even coating.

recipes cake, binding *techniques* shaping, chocolate & coatings, dipping, glitters

cake heaven

You'll be in heaven with this mouth-watering collection of cupcakes and cake slices. Any sponge base and binding can be used.

you will need...

makes 8 of each

- ♡ 8 triangular bases on sticks (30g/1oz)
- ♡ 8 cupcake-shaped pop bases on sticks (40g/1½oz)
- ♡ 300g (10½oz) each caramel, dark and milk chocolate callets, melted
- ♡ chocolate vermicelli and rainbow strands
- ♡ melted white chocolate in piping bag
- ♡ 300g (10½oz) pink candy coating, melted

For the cake slices

1 Dip each of your cake slice pops into the melted caramel chocolate and set aside to dry.

2 Carefully dip the top and outside edge of the cake slices into the melted dark chocolate and then immediately touch the wet chocolate coating into a small mound of dark chocolate vermicelli.

3 Snip off the tip of a parchment piping bag filled with a little melted white chocolate and pipe two thin lines of cream filling.

For the cupcakes

4 Dip the whole cupcake pop bases into melted milk chocolate.

5 When dry, dip the top part into the melted pink candy coating, swirl in circles above the bowl until the excess has dripped off and then turn upright. Sprinkle with rainbow sugar strands to finish.

make it special...
These little cakes are very versatile, so experiment with lots of different chocolate colour combinations for special occasions. Why not make a whole cake of 'slices'?

---

recipes cake, binding *techniques* shaping, chocolate & coatings, dipping, sprinkles & non pareils

tempting truffles

Everyone's favourite sweet treat on a stick! These truffle pops are made from Belgian chocolate and have luxurious chocolate ganache fillings.

you will need...
makes 12

- ♡ 12 round cake pop bases on sticks (30g/1oz balls) – 6 vanilla sponge with strawberry ganache and 6 devil's cake with dark chocolate ganache

- ♡ 200g (7oz) each strawberry, dark and white chocolate callets, melted

- ♡ piping bag

1 Prepare the cake pops. Dip the vanilla sponge pops into the melted strawberry chocolate and set aside to dry. Dip the devil's cake pops into the melted dark chocolate and set aside.

2 Spoon a little of the melted dark chocolate into a parchment piping bag with a tiny hole at the end. Pipe very fine drizzled lines of dark chocolate on the strawberry pops. Pipe the melted white chocolate on the dark chocolate pops. Practise the technique over the bowl of melted chocolate first.

make it special...
For a decadent adult treat, add a liqueur to your fillings. Try orange liqueur with dark ganache. Combine with devil's chocolate cake and dip into caramel chocolate.

recipes cake, binding   *techniques* chocolate & coatings, dipping

sweet treats

These luxurious pops rival a box of chocolates any day and can be used as a treat for all kinds of occasions. Create a collection of your favourite flavours and box them up in fun packaging for a gift to remember.

As with a box of chocolates, you can vary the flavours used in these cake pops. Try peanut butter or orange for children and mint chocolate or cappuccino for adults.

you will need...
makes 16

- ♡ 16 round cake pop bases on sticks (30g/1oz balls) – 4 different flavours (see step 1)

- ♡ 200g (7oz) each 4 colours of chocolate or coating, melted

- ♡ small squares of coloured foil to wrap

- ♡ small squares of clear cellophane

- ♡ curling ribbon to tie wrapping

1 Choose four different flavours from: coconut, caramel, strawberry, lemon, orange, peanut butter, mint chocolate, violet, vanilla, milk, cappuccino, white or dark chocolate. Use these flavours in your frostings, sponge bases and some of them in the finishing chocolate coating.

2 Dip four cake pops of each colour/flavour and set aside to dry.

3 When dry, wrap a sheet of coloured foil around each sweet. Add a layer of cellophane and tie in place with curling ribbon. Use the back of a pair of scissors to stroke firmly against the ribbon to create the curls. You could use multicoloured cellophane to add extra colour on top of your foil.

make it special...
You could choose the wrapping colours to suit a special wedding anniversary, such as silver, ruby, sapphire, gold or emerald.

gift box presentation
These pops would look great in a polystyrene block wrapped in pretty paper. For a really special occasion use a gift box, matching the colours to the foils you've used. Look for boxes that open up fully or those with fully detachable lids, as they are great for displaying cake pops.

recipes cake, binding *techniques* chocolate & coatings, dipping, presentation & storage

ice pops

So realistic you'll think they will melt, these delicious pops have been created as tempting ices. Ideal to eat on any day – whatever the weather.

you will need...
makes 5 of each

- ♡ 5 round cake pops and 5 rectangular pops each 45g (1¾oz) – vanilla sponge and buttercream
- ♡ 5 waffle cones
- ♡ 500g (18oz) each dark, strawberry and white chocolate or candy coating
- ♡ flaky chocolate bar broken into 5 sticks
- ♡ 5 flat wooden ice lolly sticks
- ♡ sugar sprinkles

For the ice cream pops

1 Take the chilled cake balls and push each securely into the tops of the waffle cones.

2 Melt the white chocolate and coat the pops. As it begins to firm, drizzle melted dark chocolate over. Insert a piece of flaky chocolate to finish.

For the ice lolly pops

3 Shape and create the rectangular cake bases at the same time, cutting them neatly at the base and rounding off the top. Insert a lolly stick into the base of each rectangular pop. Remove the sticks. Place on baking parchment and chill.

4 Melt the white chocolate and pour a little into a parchment piping bag. Snip off the tip, pipe the chocolate into a hole and then replace the stick. Repeat for all the lollies and refrigerate for a few minutes.

5 Dip each lolly into the white chocolate, coating down to the stick (re-melting if required). Lift out, rotate to remove the excess and place in a polystyrene block until touch dry.

6 Melt the strawberry coating. Dip into the strawberry coating to cover two-thirds and then into the sugar sprinkles to finish. You can change the colour order of the coatings used.

---

recipes cake, binding *techniques* chocolate & coatings, dipping, sprinkles & non pareils

perfect presents

These pops, like sweet little presents waiting to be unwrapped, are perfect for every occasion and are great fun to make.

you will need...

makes 12

- 12 square cake pop bases on sticks (40g/1½oz) – see step 1
- 400g (14oz) each white and dark chocolate callets, melted
- modelling paste in pink, yellow, green, red, blue, orange
- royal icing in small piping bag
- small circle plunger cutter

1 For the pops, use chocolate buttermilk cake with chocolate buttercream.

2 Dip half the pops into the melted white chocolate and set aside to dry. Dip the remaining pops into the dark chocolate and set aside to dry.

3 Roll out the modelling paste thinly and cut two narrow strips for each pop. Use royal icing in a small piping bag with the tip snipped off to apply them to the pops, crossing them over at the top. Make a bow for each gift.

4 Make the ribbon curls by cutting thin strips of paste and winding them around a pop stick, as shown right. Attach the ribbon curls to the parcels with royal icing.

5 Cut out small circles with the plunger cutter and apply to the sides of some of the pops. Use the same methods to create your second set of parcel colours.

---

recipes cake, binding   *techniques* chocolate & coatings, dipping, decorating & modelling, making bows

romantic moments

love hearts

You will know you are loved if you receive these romantic red and dark chocolate hearts. Each one is decorated with stunning golden icing detail.

you will need...
makes 12

- ♡ **12 heart-shaped cake pop bases on sticks (40g/1½oz)** – red velvet cake base and vanilla buttercream coloured red
- ♡ **200g (7oz) dark chocolate callets, melted**
- ♡ **200g (7oz) red candy melts, melted**
- ♡ **100g (3½oz) royal icing in piping bag with no. 1.5 nozzle**
- ♡ **gold edible lustre dust**

1 Dip six pops into each colour of melted coating and leave to dry.

2 Use the royal icing in a parchment piping bag with a no. 1.5 nozzle to pipe your heart/swirl design on to the front of each cake pop. Set aside to dry. Our designs were inspired by Bollywood henna patterns.

3 Mix a little gold edible lustre dust with some isopropyl alcohol or any clear alcohol to a smooth paint. Using a no. 2 sable paintbrush, apply the gold to the piped work, following the pattern and taking care not to get any on the lower surface of the cake pop.

smooth and golden...
If your gold paint becomes dry and is turning back to lustre dust, add more alcohol to keep it as a smooth liquid to paint with.

---

recipes cake, binding *techniques* shaping, chocolate & coatings, dipping, using royal icing, lustre dusts

pretty posies

Instead of a posy of flowers, say 'thank you' or 'I love you' with a bouquet of sweet pops. These are sure to be received with great delight!

you will need...
makes 12

- ♡ 12 round cake pop bases on sticks (30g/1oz balls) – red velvet cake base with lemon cream cheese frosting
- ♡ 300g (10½oz) dark chocolate callets, melted
- ♡ 12 sugar daisy decorations in bright colours with contrasting centres
- ♡ edible glitter

1 You can use ready-made daisies on these pops or create your own multicoloured flowers from flower paste and flower-shaped cutters. Use contrasting colours in the centres for best effect.

2 Dip each of your pops into the melted dark chocolate and before they set top each with a single daisy flower. Edible glue could also be used to stick the flowers in place.

3 Use a fluffy paintbrush to apply a dusting of glitter to all the cake pops for a magical effect!

make it special...
There are many flower cutters available, so you could change the flowers to suit the season, such as violets for spring and marguerites for summer.

---

recipes cake, binding *techniques* chocolate & coatings, dipping, making flowers, glitters

little devils

This cute little chap is a sign of romance in the air, so why not combine him with some heart-shaped pops or glittered flowers?

you will need...
makes 12

- 12 cake pop bases (30g/1oz balls) – devil's cake and dark chocolate ganache
- 500g (18oz) red candy coating
- piping bag
- 12 lollipop sticks
- flower paste in white, black, red
- black royal icing in piping bag with no. 1.5 nozzle
- red edible glitter

1 Melt a little of the red candy coating, put into a piping bag and snip off the tip of the bag. Insert a lollipop stick into the base of a cake ball, remove and pipe melted coating into the hole. Replace the stick. Repeat for all the pops and refrigerate for a few minutes.

2 Using flower paste, roll twenty-four tiny white balls and flatten for eyes. Roll twelve black balls for noses. Roll twenty-four horns by taking a round ball of red flower paste and rolling it until it tapers. Roll twelve little sausages of red paste, pinch each in half and flatten to create a heart-shaped forked end for the tails.

3 Re-melt the red coating if needed and coat as far as the stick. As it just begins to firm, attach the eyes, nose, mouth and horns. Fix with edible glue if necessary. Pipe pupils with black royal icing.

4 Using black flower paste, roll a long sausage. Attach it with edible glue around the stick base, curling it up around the back of the cake pop. Attach a heart-shaped end to the tail. Paint edible glue on the horns and heart and tap on edible glitter with a brush to finish.

---

recipes cake, binding *techniques* chocolate & coatings, dipping, decorating & modelling, glitters

with this ring...

This selection is perfect for an engagement. Ring boxes are wrapped up and finished with sugar ribbon, complete with box displaying an edible diamond ring!

you will need...
makes 12

- 12 cube-shaped cake pop bases on sticks (40g/1½oz) – vanilla sponge and lemon buttercream
- 400g (14oz) bright blue and 200g (7oz) white candy melts, melted
- flower paste in white and beige
- royal icing in small piping bag
- edible sugar diamond
- gold edible lustre dust

1 Dip all the cake pops into the bright blue coating. Repeat again when dry if required.

2 For nine of the boxes, dip the top quarter again to create a lid effect.

3 Roll out the white flower paste thinly and cut into narrow strips. On the nine boxes with lids, lay the strips over the top of the box and attach using royal icing in a small parchment piping bag with a no. 1.5 piping nozzle.

4 Create nine white flower paste bows with tails. Attach to each cross.

5 For the remaining three pops, dip the very top surface of the pop into white candy coating. Take care not to allow drips to run down the edges (use a cocktail stick to catch them).

6 Using light beige flower paste, create a circular clasp to hold the edible diamond and glue into place.

7 Using a no. 2 sable paintbrush, paint the beige paste with a paint formed from gold lustre dust and isopropyl or any clear alcohol.

luxurious lustre...
For a very luxurious bow, lustre the white flower paste with ice-white edible powder.

recipes cake, binding   *techniques* dipping, decorating & modelling, making bows

the happy couple

Any bridal couple would be thrilled with these pops as wedding favours for their guests. Why not attach the guest's name to each pop and use as a place setting?

you will need...

makes 6 of each

- 6 round and 6 tube-shaped cake pop bases on sticks (30g/1oz balls)
- 200g (7oz) each white and dark grey candy coating
- flower paste in ivory, light green, grey, dark grey
- ivory lustre dust
- cutters: marguerite/daisy, calyx, circles
- white royal icing in piping bag
- edible pearl balls
- narrow ivory ribbon

For the bride pops

1 For the pops, use vanilla sponge base with orange buttercream. Dip the round cake pops into the melted white candy coating.

2 For each flower ball, make twenty-two medium and six small daisy plunger blossoms in ivory flower paste, shimmered with ivory lustre dust. Attach with royal icing using a no. 1.5 nozzle. Use icing to attach a small pearl to each flower.

3 Roll out the green paste and, using the calyx cutter, create six calyxes. Thread each from the base of the cake pop up and attach with icing.

4 Beneath each calyx tie a ribbon bow, cutting the tails to neat points.

For the groom pops

5 For the pops, use chocolate sponge base with orange buttercream. Dip each tube-shaped cake pop into the melted dark grey candy coating.

6 When dry, roll out the grey flower paste and cut a 5cm (2in) circle. Use a smaller cutter to cut a circle in the centre. Thread this up the cake pop stick and attach to the base of the pop with royal icing.

7 Using the dark grey flower paste, roll a band to go around the base of the cake pop to finish the top hat.

recipes cake, binding *techniques* chocolate & coatings, dipping, decorating & modelling

wedded bliss

Two cake pops create this stunning wedding-themed arrangement. Miniature wedding cake pops are decorated with flower details and traditional royal icing, while balls covered with lilac petals resemble pretty bridal bouquets. The cake pops make a stunning centrepiece and a great alternative cake for any couple about to tie the knot.

Decorating the cake pops with piping patterns is great fun. Scallops are a classic but this is a great opportunity to get creative and make up pretty designs of your own.

you will need...

makes 24

- ♡ 12 two-tier round cake pop bases on sticks – see step 1
- ♡ 12 round cake pop balls (20g/¾oz)
- ♡ 400g (14oz) white chocolate callets, melted
- ♡ 336 rounded petal blossoms (small and medium) in lilac flower paste
- ♡ royal icing in piping bag with no. 1.5 nozzle
- ♡ 300g (10½oz) lilac candy coating, melted

For the wedding cake pops

1 The two-tier cake pop bases are 30g (1oz) circles for the base tier and 10g (⅓oz) for the top tier, each 1cm (⅜in) deep. Use vanilla or coconut sponge with lemon buttercream.

2 Dip the wedding cake pops in melted white chocolate and allow to dry.

3 Attach a selection of lilac blossoms to the top tier with a little royal icing. Use various combinations.

4 Decorate the sides of the tiers with delicate piping detail using royal icing in a parchment piping bag with a no. 1.5 nozzle.

For the flower ball pops

5 Use vanilla or coconut sponge with lemon buttercream.

6 Dip the flower balls in the lilac candy coating and allow to dry.

7 Attach various sizes of petal blossoms to the flower balls with royal icing and dot each centre with icing.

---

recipes cake, binding *techniques* chocolate & coatings, dipping, using royal icing

wedding presentation

You can create a really lovely presentation for these gorgeous wedding pops quite easily and turn them into a stunning centrepiece. We iced two round polystyrene cake dummies and trimmed them with wide lilac ribbon to act as a base to display the wedding cake pops.

new baby

sweet feet

Irresistible pastel-coloured sugar feet complete with tiny toes decorate these simple heart-shaped pops – a tasty gift to welcome a new baby into the family.

you will need...
makes 12

- ♡ 12 heart-shaped cake pop bases on sticks (40g/1½oz) – vanilla, lemon or coconut sponge and vanilla buttercream
- ♡ flower paste in pale pink, lilac, baby blue
- ♡ 350g (12oz) white chocolate callets, melted

1 Knead your first colour of flower paste and roll six pea-size balls. Add pressure to one side and roll until it is tear-drop shaped. Flatten this to resemble a foot outline, bending one to the left and one to the right for a pair of feet. Roll six sets of five small balls for toes, graduating them in size. Repeat this modelling with all the flower paste colours.

2 Dip each heart-shaped pop into the melted white chocolate, double dipping if required to get a smooth coating. Apply the centre of the foot shape to the wet chocolate and put aside to set.

3 When dry, use a no. 4 paintbrush to apply a line of sugar glue above the top of the foot. Glue on the toes, spacing them out evenly, to finish.

go easy with tiny toes...
Picking up tiny sugar toes is difficult with fingers or a palette knife, so use a slightly damp brush to position the toes in the right place.

---

recipes cake, binding *techniques* using flower paste, dipping

party teddies

Everyone will love these adorable teddies decorated with glittered pink and blue bows – perfect for birthday parties. Simple tools create a realistic teddy look.

you will need...
makes 10

- ♡ **10 round cake pop bases on sticks (30g/1oz balls)**
- ♡ **flower paste in caramel, cream, dark brown, baby pink and blue**
- ♡ **stitching/quilting, ball and smile tools**
- ♡ **300g (10½oz) caramel chocolate callets, melted**
- ♡ **edible glitters in baby pink and blue**
- ♡ **black royal icing in small piping bag with no. 1 nozzle**

1 For the pops, use chocolate sponge with caramel buttercream.

2 For ears, roll five small balls of caramel flower paste. Flatten slightly and insert a ball tool in the centre to create a dip. Cut each in half.

3 For a muzzle, roll ten small balls of cream flower paste. Flatten slightly and impress with a smile tool on the lower half. Roll ten small dark brown balls for noses.

4 Create five small bows in baby pink and five in baby blue.

5 Dip your pops into the melted caramel chocolate and

attach the ears while still wet. When touch dry, draw a 'stitching' line from the back of the head over the top between the ears and down to the centre front. Attach the muzzle and nose with glue. When dry, pipe eyes with black icing using a no. 1 nozzle.

6 Use edible glue to attach pink bows to the top of the girl bears' heads, slightly to one side. Glue blue bows under the chin of all the boy bears.

practise makes perfect...
Practise with the stitching tool first to ensure you get an even depth when you press into the cake pop.

---

recipes cake, binding *techniques* chocolate & coatings, dipping, decorating & modelling

dotty for you

A beautiful bouquet of cute pops is a fun and tasty gift. Celebrate a new baby with pastel-coloured bows, flowers and polka dots.

you will need...
makes 16

- ♡ 16 round cake pop bases on sticks (30g/1oz balls) – see step 1
- ♡ 200g (7oz) each pink, lemon, mid-blue, light green candy coating
- ♡ edible shimmer dusts in baby pink, lemon, ice-white
- ♡ flower paste in pale blue, baby pink, lemon
- ♡ cutters: blossom plunger, circle
- ♡ white royal icing

1 For the pops, use a vanilla base with lemon cream cheese frosting. Dip four cake pops into each melted candy coating colour and set aside to dry. Apply matching shimmer dust with a dry dusting brush. Dust the green with ice-white shimmer but omit the shimmer for the mid-blue.
2 Knead pale blue flower paste, roll out thinly and cut and shape to create the top section of a bow. Shimmer with ice-white and set aside to dry.
3 For flowers, roll out baby pink and lemon flower paste colours. Use a blossom plunger cutter to cut out about nine per pop. Leave to dry.

4 Pipe centres of white royal icing on the flowers using a piping bag with a no. 1 nozzle. When dry, use sugar glue to stick the flowers around the lemon and baby pink pops.
5 Roll out pale blue paste and cut small circles (about nineteen per pop). Dust with ice-white shimmer and, while soft, attach each circle to the pale green pops with glue.
6 Roll out more pale blue paste, create tails for the bows and shimmer. While still soft, attach to the mid-blue pops, adjusting into a flowing shape. Use sugar glue to attach the top section of the bow on to the tails.

recipes cake, binding *techniques* chocolate & coatings, dipping, decorating & modelling

hush, baby

Could there be a cuter way to celebrate a new baby than with these candy-coloured pops in the shape of a soothing dummy? Made of delicious lemon sponge with cream cheese frosting, they are sure to please children and adults alike. Finish each with different coloured bases and decorate with stars.

These dummies were decorated with tiny stars using a mini star cutter, but there are many other shapes available for you to use — try little hearts or flowers.

- ♡ **12 lozenge-shaped cake pop bases on sticks (30g/1oz) – see step 1**

- ♡ **300g (10½oz) white chocolate callets, melted**

- ♡ **flower paste in lemon, baby blue, light pink, white and bright pink (to match presentation bucket)**

- ♡ **circle cutters: 6cm (2⅜in), 1cm (⅜in) and 4cm (1½in)**

- ♡ **mini star plunger cutter**

- ♡ **royal icing in piping bag with no. 1.5 nozzle**

1 For the cake pops, use lemon sponge bases with cream cheese frosting. Dip all the teat top parts of the pops in the white chocolate and leave to dry.

2 To create the lip guards, use a 6cm (2⅜in) cutter to cut out four circles of each colour of flower paste. Using a 1cm (⅜in) cutter, cut a circle in the centre of each to allow for them to thread up under the cake pop.

3 Using the star plunger cutter, cut some stars in bright pink flower paste and attach to the lip guards using edible glue and a paintbrush.

4 Thread the lip guard up to sit beneath the teat and attach with royal icing.

5 Using the 6cm (2⅜in) cutter, cut twelve circles from white flower paste. Cut out each centre with a 4cm (1½in) cutter. Set aside to dry.

6 When dry, using royal icing and a parchment piping bag with a no. 1.5 nozzle, pipe a little icing at two points, top and bottom of the rear of the circle, and then press on to the cake pop stick to attach.

baby presentation

We used this fantastic pink metal bucket as a great way to present these cake pop dummies. Just fill the base with something heavy to hold your cake pops in place firmly (we used some sugar paste) and then scatter coloured sugar on the top surface. Position your cake pops for maximum effect.

recipes cake, binding **techniques** chocolate & coatings, dipping, decorating & modelling

seasonal style

spring chicks

This sweet little fellow is just popping out of his shell and makes a really cute cake pop design to welcome spring or for Easter celebrations.

you will need...
makes 9

- ♡ 9 cake pop bases (50g/1¾oz balls) moulded into hourglass shapes (see step 1) – vanilla sponge and buttercream
- ♡ 500g (18oz) yellow candy coating
- ♡ 8 lollipop sticks
- ♡ flower paste in yellow, marigold orange
- ♡ black royal icing in piping bag
- ♡ white modelling paste

1 An hourglass shape is made by rolling two fingers either side of the centre of the ball. Place on baking parchment and chill to firm.

2 Melt the yellow candy coating, pour a little into a piping bag and snip off the tip of the bag. Insert a lollipop stick into a cake ball base, remove and pipe the melted coating into the hole. Push the stick back into the hole. Repeat for all the pops and refrigerate for a few minutes.

3 For wings, knead the yellow flower paste and create flattened oval shapes. Roll little points of marigold orange flower paste for beaks.

4 Dip the pops into the yellow candy coating, re-melting the candy coating if needed.

5 As the coating firms, attach the beak and wings, fixing with edible glue if necessary. Pipe eyes with black royal icing and a no. 1 nozzle.

6 For the eggshell, create a ball of white modelling paste, flatten to a circle and cut points all round. Hold the circle under the cake pop and thread on to the stick. Dab sugar glue on the upper surface of the shell and ease on to the bottom of the cake pop. Add a little shell piece to some of the chicks' heads.

recipes cake, binding   *techniques* shaping, chocolate & coatings, dipping, decorating & modelling

funny bunnies

Everyone will be hopping with delight with this Easter treat! Give the bunnies different expressions by changing the faces, ear colours and eye positions.

you will need...
makes 8

- ♡ 8 round cake pop bases on sticks (30g/1oz balls) – any sponge and binding
- ♡ flower paste in white, black, pale pink
- ♡ cutters: small round plunger and small heart plunger
- ♡ light brown edible pen
- ♡ 300g (10½oz) cappuccino chocolate callets, melted

1 Using white flower paste, make sixteen tiny balls, flattened for eyes. Cut small black circles of flower paste with a plunger cutter and glue on to the eyes with edible glue.

2 Using white flower paste, make sixteen pea-size balls for cheeks, squished together in pairs and dotted with light brown edible pen.

3 Using white flower paste, make eight sets of teeth, making a line down the centre to mark them into two. Model sixteen ears.

4 Using pale pink flower paste, cut out eight heart-shaped noses. Model sixteen pink ear centres and attach to the white ears with glue.

5 Now dip the cake pops into the melted cappuccino callets and immediately decorate with the ears, eyes, cheeks and teeth.

sticky fingers...
Use sugar glue to attach additional features if your chocolate coating has dried too quickly.

recipes cake, binding *techniques* chocolate & coatings, dipping, embellishments

hallowe'en fun

Scary ghosts and party pumpkin pops make excellent Hallowe'en treats – unless you prefer a trick of course! These cake pops will thrill parents and kids alike.

you will need...
makes 12 of each

- ♡ 12 round and 12 pumpkin-shaped cake pop bases on sticks (30g/1oz balls)
- ♡ 300g (10½oz) each black and orange candy melts, melted
- ♡ white modelling paste
- ♡ cutters: large and tiny round, daisy
- ♡ flower paste in black, green, mid-brown
- ♡ black royal icing in piping bag

For the ghosts

1 For the pops, use red velvet cake or chocolate sponge with chocolate buttercream. Dip your pops into the melted black candy melts.

2 Roll out the white modelling paste and cut out circles with a large cutter. Starting below the centre, use a small plunger cutter to cut two eye holes and a mouth. Wiggle the cutter to elongate the holes.

3 Sugar glue the paste circle on the pop, flat against the surface. Bring the white sides outwards and push the front and back parts together to form the arms of the ghost. Add glue between the two if required.

For the pumpkins

4 For the pops, use zesty orange sponge with orange buttercream.

5 Roll out black flower paste and cut out twenty-four small triangles for eyes with a palette knife.

6 Roll out and cut twelve small green flowers with a daisy cutter. Press a dip in the centre and leave to dry.

7 Dip the pops in the melted orange candy melts and attach the green flowers to the tops while still wet.

8 Roll twelve medium balls of brown paste into cone shapes. Glue to the green tops. When touch dry, glue on the eyes. Pipe a black zigzag mouth in royal icing with a no. 1.5 nozzle.

recipes cake, binding *techniques* chocolate & coatings, dipping, decorating & modelling

spooky sponges

Hallowe'en wouldn't be the same without night creatures like these beastly bats, but kids will probably pick the ghoulish eyeballs!

you will need...
makes 12 of each

- ♡ 12 round cake pop bases on sticks (30g/1oz) for bats and 12 for eyeballs
- ♡ flower paste in white, black, green
- ♡ cutters: round plunger, holly leaf
- ♡ 300g (10½oz) black candy melts, melted
- ♡ black royal icing in piping bag
- ♡ red food colouring
- ♡ black edible pen and clear gel

For the bats

1 For the pops, use red velvet sponge with strawberry buttercream.
2 Cut out twenty-four small circles of white flower paste, flattened for eyes. Cut twenty-four triangles for teeth.
3 Roll out black flower paste to medium thickness and cut twenty-four wings with a holly leaf cutter.
4 Dip the pops into melted black candy melts and fasten a pair of wings to each. Use edible glue to attach the eyes and teeth. Use black royal icing and a no. 1.5 nozzle to pipe pupils on the eyes. Use a paintbrush to apply red food colouring to the teeth and cake base so it dribbles down the stick.

For the eyeballs

5 For the pops, use lemon sponge with lemon cream cheese frosting. Dip the pops and set aside to dry.
6 Roll a large ball of green flower paste and flatten for the iris of the eye. Roll a medium ball of black flower paste and flatten for the pupil. Attach to the iris and draw lines out from the centre with a black pen. Attach the iris and pupil combination to your pop. Paint the whole eye with edible clear gel.
7 With a clean brush, add clear gel to the red colouring and paint red lines through the gel to create the bloodshot effect.

recipes cake, binding *techniques* chocolate & coatings, dipping, decorating & modelling

christmas treats

What festive fun will be had with these great holiday treats! Decorated Christmas trees and jolly Santa hats make wonderful gifts for family and friends.

you will need...

makes 12 of each

- 24 cone-shaped cake pop bases on sticks (40g/1½oz balls), curving 12 for hats
- orange flower paste
- small star cutter
- 300g (10½oz) each green and red candy melts, melted
- gold and silver edible balls
- gold edible lustre dust
- white royal icing
- hologram hint of violet sparkly glitter

For the Christmas trees

1 For the pops, use vanilla sponge with orange buttercream.

2 Cut out twelve star shapes from orange flower paste. Dip the pops into the green candy melts and sprinkle with gold and silver balls. Attach a star to the top of each tree.

3 When the surface has firmed, add a little isopropyl alcohol or any clear alcohol to the lustre dust and paint the stars gold.

all that glitters...
If glitter strays on to the red parts, use a slightly damp brush to lift it away.

For the Santa hats

4 For the pops, use red velvet sponge with strawberry ganache. Remember to curve the pops to create hat shapes.

5 Dip the pops into the red candy melts and leave to firm.

6 Snip the end from a parchment piping bag of white royal icing and pipe a ball at the tip of the hat and around the hat base. Use rough up and down motions so that the icing looks fluffy. When the icing hardens, paint edible glue on to it.

7 Dip a fluffy pony-hair brush into the glitter and tap it over the glue on the white parts of the hat to finish.

---

recipes cake, binding   *techniques* chocolate & coatings, dipping, decorating & modelling, glitters

festive snowstorm

What a lovely winter centrepiece this sugar snowstorm would make for a Christmas or New Year celebration. There are two different pops: one featuring Santa's faithful reindeers, linked together by festive red ribbon, and the other decorated with delicate snowflakes.

The decoration on the snowflake cake pops is made from white flower paste cut out with a snowflake cutter. This is then dusted beautifully with edible glitter.

you will need...

makes 24

- ♡ 12 round cake pop bases on sticks (40g/1½oz balls) – see step 1
- ♡ 12 round cake pop bases on sticks (30g/1oz balls) – see step 5
- ♡ 400g (14oz) each milk and white chocolate callets, melted
- ♡ jelly sweets and mini pretzels
- ♡ black and white royal icing in 2 piping bags
- ♡ red and white edible glitter and ice-white edible shimmer lustre dust
- ♡ white flower paste
- ♡ snowflake plunger cutters in 3 sizes

glitter sense...

Placing the snowflakes on some baking parchment when you glitter them means you will be able to funnel the excess loose glitter back into the pot.

For the reindeer pops

1 For twelve of the pop bases, use chocolate sponge with chocolate ganache. Dip in the melted milk chocolate and set aside to dry.

2 For noses, use a no. 4 sable paintbrush to paint twelve jelly sweets with edible glue and then liberally apply red edible glitter using a fluffy no. 8 pony-hair brush.

3 Attach the noses to the front of the pops with black royal icing. Use the black royal icing in a piping bag with a no. 1.5 nozzle to pipe eyes.

4 Break a pretzel for an antler and push into position in the top of the pop.

---

recipes cake, binding *techniques* chocolate & coatings, dipping, decorating & modelling, embellishments

For the snowflake pops

5 For the remaining pop bases, use vanilla sponge with vanilla buttercream. Dip the pops in the melted white chocolate and allow to dry. Apply ice-white edible shimmer lustre dust with a wide dusting brush.
6 Roll out white flower paste and use the snowflake plunger cutters to cut a variety of sizes. When dry, paint with sugar glue and use a dry fluffy brush to apply white edible glitter. Tap off the excess glitter and attach to the white cake pops with white royal icing.

snowstorm presentation

For this festive snowstorm we took two polystyrene cake dummies and completely coated them in fluffy royal icing, which we then dusted with amazing edible glitter. Dot the royal icing with any spare snowflakes to add to the wintery effect.

seasonal snowmen

Here's a snowman with style — check out the polka dot scarf! Serve these at a festive gathering and hearts will be melting rather than snowmen.

you will need...
makes 12

- 💜 12 double-ball cake pop bases on sticks (15g/½oz and 40g/1½oz balls)
- 💜 400g (14oz) white candy melts, melted
- 💜 modelling paste in red and lilac
- 💜 round plunger cutter
- 💜 marigold flower paste
- 💜 black royal icing in small piping bag with no. 1 nozzle

1 For the cake pops, use lemon sponge and lemon buttercream.

2 Dip all the pops into the melted white candy melts.

3 Roll and cut out small circles of red modelling paste using the round plunger cutter. Roll out the lilac paste to a medium thickness, pop the red circles on top of the lilac paste and roll the paste again to blend the two colours slightly.

4 Use a brush to apply sugar glue around the neck of the snowman. Cut the polka dot paste into strips and use small scissors to cut a fringe at either end. Wrap the scarf around the snowman so it sticks to the sugar glue and overlaps at the front.

5 For the nose, roll out a small cone of marigold flower paste and attach to the face with edible glue. Using black royal icing in a small parchment piping bag with a no. 1 nozzle, pipe black dots for coal eyes and your snowman is fit to party!

make it special...
If you have time, make your snowman a sweet little sugar hat to keep him cosy!

---

recipes cake, binding   *techniques* chocolate & coatings, dipping, decorating & modelling

animal friends

farmyard fun

This is my favourite of the presentation ideas — what adult or child would not love receiving a mini field of four different farm animal pops? These loveable farmyard friends are so cute they look too good to eat! For a simpler way of presenting them, wrap a polystyrene block in gift paper, leaving the top open, and coat the block's surface with green shredded tissue paper. Push the pops into place on the grassy base.

This farmyard collection of pigs, cows, sheep and chickens is made more charming by the addition of little extras, such as flowers. Add to their character and facial expressions by varying the eye positions.

you will need... makes 3 of each

- ♡ 9 round cake pops (pigs, sheep and chickens) on sticks (30g/1oz) – see step 1

- ♡ 3 flattened oval cake pop bases (cow) on sticks (40g/1½oz)

- ♡ 200g (7oz) each pink and milk chocolate

- ♡ 200g (7oz) each black and white candy coating

- ♡ tiny white sugar balls (non pareils)

- ♡ pink chocolate paste

- ♡ ball tool

- ♡ modelling paste in black, white, light brown, yellow, pink, pale pink

- ♡ black royal icing in piping bag with no. 1.5 nozzle

- ♡ cutters: small circle plunger, small daisy, graduated small hearts

1 For the pigs, sheep and chickens, use vanilla sponge and vanilla buttercream. For the cows, use lemon sponge and lemon buttercream. Melt your chocolate and coatings ready for dipping.

2 Of the nine round pops, dip three into the pink chocolate and three into the milk chocolate. Set aside to dry. Dip the remaining three round balls into the black coating and immediately coat the rear and top of the pop in tiny white sugar balls to create the sheep's head. Dip the flattened oval shapes for the cows into the white coating.

make it special...
Dress your cows up with cow bells! Simply model a pear shape, flatten slightly, and create a dip in the bottom. Leave as plain brown paste or paint with gold lustre for extra shine!

---

recipes cake, binding *techniques* chocolate & coatings, dipping, decorating & modelling

For the pigs

3 Using pink chocolate paste, model three snouts. Use a ball tool to mark nostrils. Set aside to dry. Model six ears in the same paste.

For the cows

4 Using the pink paste, model three snouts, as before. Paint random splodges on the cows with black coating. Model six teardrop shapes in black modelling paste. Attach to the head with royal icing.

5 Cut out six small circles from white modelling paste for eyes and attach to the faces.

6 Cut three daisy flowers in light brown and attach as the tuft of hair between the ears.

For the chickens

7 Model three mini cone shapes in yellow. Attach to the chicken front.

8 Cut three large, six medium and three small hearts in pink modelling paste and attach them in graduated sizes to the top of the heads. Put a medium heart beneath each chin.

9 Cut out six small circles from white modelling paste for eyes and attach to the faces.

For the sheep

10 Cut three pale pink tiny hearts for noses and attach. Roll three thin sausages of pale pink for a smile and a tiny yellow flower on one side of the smile. Cut out six small circles from white modelling paste for eyes and attach to the faces.

11 Using black royal icing, pipe pupils on all the remaining cake pop eyes.

farmyard presentation

For this presentation you will need: a 20.3cm (8in) square block of polystyrene; green sugar paste; light brown flower paste; Dresden tool; brown dusting powder; 2 shades of green royal icing in 2 piping bags with leaf nozzle (optional) and no. 1.5 nozzle (see step 3); sugar flowers.

1 Cover the block of polystyrene in rolled-out green sugar paste.

2 Roll out some light brown flower paste to a medium thickness and cut four lengths for the horizontal bars on the gate, two slightly shorter lengths for uprights and one longer section for the diagonal cross bar. Score with a Dresden tool to create a wood effect and dust with brown dusting powder to give depth. While the paste is still soft, use the end of a nozzle to mark nail holes in the paste and set aside to dry.

3 Use royal icing to fix the bars to the side of the cake and attach the uprights and cross bar. Use one shade of green royal icing and a piping bag with a leaf nozzle or V cut in the end to pipe foliage. Use the other green icing and a no. 1.5 nozzle to pipe grass. Decorate with sugar flowers to finish.

forest friends

This charming forest scene of snails, hedgehogs, toadstools and owls comes complete with a realistic log created from cake. The display makes a brilliant gift for a party and the cake log means there will be plenty to go around for everyone!

There are some great details in this forest display and you will enjoy adding extra touches, such as the toadstool spots, snail shells, owl feathers and hedgehog spines.

you will need... *makes 3 of each*

- ♡ 3 teardrop cake pops (hedgehog) on sticks (40g/1½oz) – see step 1
- ♡ 3 owl-shaped pops on sticks (40g/1½oz)
- ♡ 3 round flattened pop bases (snail) on sticks (30g/1oz)
- ♡ 3 mushroom-shaped pops on sticks (30g/1oz)
- ♡ 250g (9oz) dark chocolate, melted
- ♡ 300g (10½oz) white candy coating, melted
- ♡ 250g (9oz) each red, yellow and blue candy coating
- ♡ 200g (9oz) dark chocolate vermicelli

- ♡ modelling paste in light brown, brown, purple, lilac
- ♡ flower paste in white, pink, lilac, purple
- ♡ black, purple and light lilac royal icing in 3 piping bags
- ♡ cutters: small circle, tiny heart and blossom plunger

....

1 For the hedgehog and owl pops, use devil's cake and ganache. For the snails and mushrooms, use vanilla sponge and vanilla buttercream. Melt the chocolate and coatings for dipping.

For the hedgehogs

2 Trim off the pointed end from a teardrop pop. Dip into the dark

chocolate and then into chocolate vermicelli for a spiky coating.

3 Model a pointed snout in light brown modelling paste and attach. Roll a little ball of brown modelling paste for a nose and attach with black royal icing in a parchment bag with a no. 1.5 nozzle. Pipe on black dots for eyes.

---

recipes cake, binding   *techniques* shaping, chocolate & coatings, dipping, decorating & modelling

For the mushrooms

4 Dip the whole mushroom shape into the white coating. Once touch dry, dip the top into the red coating but only to the edge. Using a small circle cutter, cut circles from white flower paste and glue lots over the surface. Reduce the pop stick lengths so they sit nearer the forest floor.

For the snails

5 Dip the round snail shell into yellow candy coating and set aside to dry.
6 Shape a sausage in purple/lilac modelling paste for the head, body and tail. Thread this up the stick and glue on the underside of the shell. Glue the head up at the front.
7 Add white flower paste circles and black dots on the eyes. Pipe a spiral on the shell with purple royal icing.

For the owls

8 The pop shape is an oval with the top slightly indented and shaped upwards to create little pointed ears. Dip into the blue coating.
9 Form a teardrop shape from pink flower paste for wings. Flatten it and, with a palette knife, score at one edge for feathers and attach.
10 Cut out tiny flower paste hearts in lilac, purple, white and pink for chest feathers. Cut out two pink blossoms and squish together to become the tuft on the head. Cut two small and two mid-sized hearts for feet.
11 For eyes, use the cutters to cut pink blossoms and a white circle for the centre. Pipe purple royal icing around the edge and fill with piped light lilac royal icing. Dot with black royal icing for the pupils.

woodland presentation

For this presentation you will need: a cake board; a 25.5cm (10in) square chocolate sponge 6.5cm (2½in) high; chocolate buttercream or ganache; sugar paste in chocolate brown and green; cake smoother; Dresden tool; CMC powder (carboxylmethyl cellulose); wooden skewer or cake pop stick; edible gel; green royal icing in piping bag with no. 1.5 nozzle; multicoloured flower paste blossoms; narrow green ribbon; double-sided adhesive tape.

1 Cut the sponge in half and put one half on top of the other. Carve the top and side edges into a rounded log shape. Layer and fill with chocolate buttercream or ganache.

2 Cover the cake with chocolate brown sugar paste. Cover one end up neatly. Pleat the other end upwards to create an open end. Smooth the main part of the cake with a cake smoother. At the covered end, cut a round shape from the paste and use a Dresden tool to mark concentric circles. Use the tool on the surface to score a wood effect. On the open end, work the paste into a jagged effect.

3 Take lumps of spare sugar paste and place on the cake board. Roll out green sugar paste and cover over the lumps to create an undulating forest floor.

4 Take some chocolate brown sugar paste, knead in some CMC powder to create a modelling paste and when firm shape into a branch. For the upper branch, insert a wooden skewer or cake pop stick into the base while still soft to anchor it into the log when firm. Do the same for a smaller side branch and fix both to the log.

5 Place a hedgehog in the open end of the log, cutting the stick to fit. Put a snail at the top of the smaller branch and an owl near the larger branch. Dot the mushrooms about on the forest floor. Paint a trail of edible gel behind the snail.

6 Pipe grass with squiggles of green royal icing. Cut out multicoloured flower paste blossoms for the forest floor.

7 Finish by attaching narrow green ribbon to the edge of the silver cake board with double-sided adhesive tape.

suppliers

Cakes 4 Fun
100 Lower Richmond Road,
Putney, London SW15 1LN
Tel: 020 8785 9039
Email: info@cakes4fun.co.uk
www.cakes4funshop.co.uk
Bespoke cake creations, sugarcraft
shop stocking all cake pop-making
equipment used in this book and
pre-mixed Devil's Cake; Sugarcraft
School teaching cake decoration
and how to create cake pops;
online shop too

Keylink Ltd
Green Lane, Ecclesfield,
Sheffield, S35 9WY
Tel: 01142 455400
www.keylink.org
Suppliers of chocolate, fillings,
decorations and packaging for the
chocolate and patisserie industry

Knightsbridge PME Ltd
Unit 23, Riverwalk Road
(off Jeffreys Road),
Enfield EN3 7QN
Tel: 020 323 40049
www.cakedecoration.co.uk
Suppliers of plunger cutters
and UK distributor of Wilton
Industries products

Tracey's Cakes Ltd
5 Wheelwright Road, Longwick,
Princes Risborough,
Bucks HP27 9ST
Tel: 01844 347147
www.traceyscakes.co.uk
Manufacturer of chocolate paste

Global Sugar Art
625 Route 3, Unit 3,
Plattsburgh, NY 12901
Tel: + 1 518 561 3039
www.globalsugarart.com
Suppliers of cake-making and
decorating equipment and materials

Kemper Enterprises, inc
13595 12th Street,
Chino, CA 91710
Tel: + 1 909 627 6191
www.kempertools.com
For mini plunger cutters and palette
knives – also available through all
good cake-decorating stores

Wilton Industries
2240 West 75th Street,
Woodridge, IL 60517
Tel: + 1 800 794 5866
www.wilton.com
Suppliers of candy melts and
cake pop-making equipment
and packaging

about the author

Carolyn's sense of fun shows through in all her work. She started her cake-making business at home following redundancy and quickly grew it through her passion for fun novelty cakes and her eye for detail. From her shop and online store, her cake business now encompasses novelty cakes, wedding and corporate cakes, cake-decorating supplies and a thriving tutoring business teaching cake enthusiasts every style of cake decorating, from cake pops to 3D designer handbags.

acknowledgments

Many thanks to the whole David & Charles team for their amazing professional approach, enthusiasm and support throughout the whole process – special thanks to James, Alison, Sarah, Jenny and Jeni. Thanks also to Sian and Joe for their fantastic photography, and to Lin and Jo for their patient editing and attention to detail.

I would also like to say a special thank you to my team at Cakes 4 Fun, in particular Penelope, Elyse, Katherine, Lisa, Rachel and Fiona for all their help with the creation of the many beautiful pops within the book.

I would also like to thank Graham, my husband, who without his inspiration, support and, more importantly, his keen accountant's eye on the always-important bottom line, the business and therefore this book would never have existed!

index

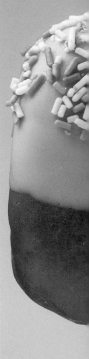

loved this book?

Tell us what you think and download a free project.

www.bakeme.com/page/love-this-book

Bake Me I'm Yours...
Whoopie Pies
Natalie Saville & Jill Collins
ISBN-13: 978-1-4463-0068-8

Over 70 great excuses to bake, fill and decorate these tempting treats! Includes everything you need to create stunning whoopie pies for your special occasions.

Bake Me I'm Yours...
Cupcake Celebration
Lindy Smith
ISBN-13: 978-0-7153-3770-7

Celebrate in style, with over 25 irresistible cupcake ideas. Add that special touch to every occasion following the beautiful designs and delicious recipes.

Bake Me I'm Yours...
Christmas
Various
ISBN-13: 978-1-4463-0060-2

A festive collection of over 20 tempting projects, which give the perfect excuse to bake at Christmas. With ideas for edible decorations and gifts that will delight your guests!

Bake Me I'm Yours...
Cupcake Love
Zoe Clark
ISBN-13: 978-0-7153-3781-3

An indulgent collection of cupcake projects, recipes and ideas for every romantic occasion. Tempt loved ones with the 20 gorgeous designs.

All details correct at time of printing.

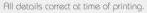